NATURE'S CHILDREN

TIGERS

by Vicky Franchino

Children's Press®

An Imprint o

New York Toronto L

Mexico City Ne

Danbury,

Content Consultant
Dr. Stephen S. Ditchkoff
Professor of Wildlife Sciences
Auburn University
Auburn, Alabama

Photographs 2013: age fotostock: 40 (R. Wittek/Arco Images), 12
(Tao Images); Alamy Images/Juniors Bildarchiv/F279: 1; Bob Italiano:
44 foreground, 45 foreground; Corbis Images/Pallava Bagla/
Sygma: 39; Dreamstime: 20 (Ankevanwyk), 23 (Nick.biemans), 2
background, 3 background, 44 background, 45 background (Oleg
Pidodnya), 2 foreground, 3 foreground, 46 (Xvaldes); iStockphoto/
Bernhard Richter: 8; Media Bakery/View Stock: 11; Photo
Researchers: 28 (D. Lepp), 31 (G. Dimijian, M.D.); Shutterstock, Inc.:
27 (Bork), 7 (Helen E. Grose), 19 (Justin Black), 24 (Nick Biemans),
5 top, 15 (red-feniks), 4, 5 background, 32 (Timothy Craig Lubcke),
36 (Yatigra); Superstock, Inc.: cover (Minden Pictures), 5 bottom, 16,
35 (NHPA).

Library of Congress Cataloging-in-Publication Data
Franchino, Vicky.
    Tigers/by Vicky Franchino.
        p. cm.—(Nature's children)
    Includes bibliographical references and index.
    ISBN-13: 978-0-531-26839-1 (lib. bdg.)
    ISBN-13: 978-0-531-25484-4 (pbk.)
    1. Tiger—Juvenile literature. I. Title.
    QL737.C23F73 2012
    599.756—dc23   2012000632

All rights reserved. Published in 2013 by Children's Press, an imprint
of Scholastic Inc.
Printed in China 62
SCHOLASTIC, CHILDREN'S PRESS, and associated logos are
trademarks and/or registered trademarks of Scholastic Inc.

1 2 3 4 5 6 7 8 9 10 R 22 21 20 19 18 17 16 15 14 13

Tigers

Class	Mammalia
Order	Carnivora
Family	Felidae
Genus	Panthera
Species	Panthera tigris
World distribution	India, China, Russian Far East, and Southeast Asia
Habitat	Grasslands and a wide range of forest environments, from hot, humid rain forests to cold, snowy coniferous forests
Distinctive physical characteristics	Largest animal in the cat family; most have orange fur with black stripes and white markings on their faces, though there are also white tigers
Habits	Solitary, except when a female is caring for cubs; sleep a large part of the day; spend many of their waking hours hunting
Diet	Large animals such as boar, antelope, and deer; have also been known to eat smaller animals and occasionally even humans

Contents

CHAPTER 1

The World's Biggest Cats

Powerful and enormous, tigers are the largest cats in the world. They are very strong and use their bone-crushing teeth to kill bear and buffalo, which are twice their size. Tigers usually weigh between 200 and 700 pounds (90 and 318 kilograms).

Tigers survive in many different **climates**. They stalk **prey** in the hot and humid rain forests and climb the snowy mountains of the Himalayas. These big cats are found throughout the **continent** of Asia and in the Russian Far East.

Warm-blooded and covered with fur, tigers are mammals. They are also **vertebrates**, which means they have a backbone.

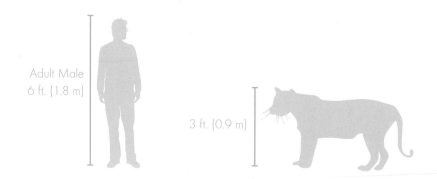

Adult Male
6 ft. (1.8 m)

3 ft. (0.9 m)

Tigers grow larger than any other cat species.

Legs, Paws, and Claws

Tigers have extremely powerful legs. These strong legs help them run up to 35 miles (56 kilometers) per hour for short periods of time. Tigers also use their legs to jump as high as 15 feet (5 meters) and as far as 32 feet (10 m).

These legs end in padded paws that enable tigers to move quietly through the jungle. Tiger paws might look soft and cuddly, but they are actually dangerous weapons. Each paw has several long, sharp claws. The claws are about 4 inches (10 centimeters) long. They help tigers hold on to their prey during an attack. They are also used for climbing. Tigers retract their claws into their paws when they aren't using them.

Unlike most cats, tigers like to swim. They use their big paws to move quickly through the water. It is not unusual to see tigers cooling off at water holes on hot days.

Tigers can easily jump over obstacles.

Mighty Hunters

Tigers are carnivores, which means they have meat as a regular part of their diet. Their favorite foods are large animals such as deer, antelope, and boar. They sometimes eat smaller animals, too.

Tigers hunt and kill their food. They rely on the element of surprise to catch fast animals. They pounce on their prey and kill it by biting into its neck. A tiger's teeth and jaws are so powerful they can snap bones in a single bite.

Tigers usually attack their prey from behind or from the side. In the Sundarbans, an area in the countries of Bangladesh and India, there are very fierce tigers that have been known to attack humans. People living in the Sundarbans wear masks on the back of their head when they go into the forest. The masks make it look like they have a face on both sides of the head. Tigers don't attack because they can't tell which way the people are facing.

Tigers sometimes eat smaller animals such as ducks.

Big Eaters

Tigers need to eat a lot of food to survive. It's not unusual for a tiger to eat more than 100 pounds (45 kg) of meat in one week. Tigers are skilled hunters, but they only succeed at catching prey about one out of every 10 to 20 times they go hunting. Because they need so much food and most of their hunts are not successful, tigers spend most of their time hunting.

When a tiger does have a successful hunt, it stuffs itself with fresh meat. It uses its strong jaws and 30 teeth to tear off chunks of meat and swallow them whole. Then it uses its rough, hooked tongue to scrape the bones clean. Tigers hide the leftover meat under piles of branches and leaves for another day.

FUN FACT! Tigers' longest teeth grow to be about 2.5 to 3 inches (6.4 to 7.6 cm) on average.

Tigers eat as much as they can at each meal.

Looking at a Tiger

It is easy to recognize tigers. Their distinct appearance makes them stand out from other animals. Most tigers have orange fur with black stripes, but each one is unique. No two tigers have the same pattern of stripes—just as no two humans have the same fingerprints. Most tigers have yellow eyes. The rare white Bengal tiger has dark stripes and blue eyes.

Looking at a tiger can also provide a good idea of what it is thinking. A loosely hanging tail means the tiger is relaxed. A tail that is swishing back and forth means the tiger is getting ready to attack. Tigers hold their tails high in the air when meeting one another in a friendly way. They hold their tails low when trying to scare off enemies. Tigers also rely on their long, flexible tails to help them balance as they chase prey through the jungle.

The white Bengal's color makes it easy to tell them apart from other types of tigers.

CHAPTER 2

Stalking Through the Forest

Many animals use **camouflage** to conceal themselves from **predators**. Healthy adult tigers are so strong, swift, and fierce that they don't have to worry about being attacked. The only time tigers need to hide from predators is when they are **cubs**.

Adult tigers use their camouflage to hide and surprise their prey. Orange and black might not seem like good colors for camouflage, but they are. The tiger's coloring, combined with the striped pattern of its fur, helps it disappear in tall grass or forest underbrush. Tigers usually hunt at night. Their fur makes them almost invisible at this time.

Tigers blend in very well with their surroundings.

Touching and Tasting

Tigers have different types of whiskers on their head, the backs of their front legs, and scattered around their body. They are much longer and thicker than regular hairs. The whiskers on a tiger's face are about 6 inches (15 cm) long. They are also rooted deeper into the skin than normal hairs are. This makes them more sensitive to touch. As a tiger moves through the jungle, its whiskers stick out and brush up against leaves, twigs, or other objects. This lets the tiger know that something is close to its face. Then it can move to avoid getting poked in the eye.

Tigers can tell the difference between some tastes, but they have very few taste buds compared to people. Taste is not very important to them. They have even been known to eat rotten meat!

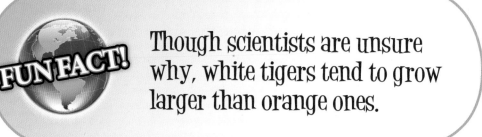

FUN FACT! Though scientists are unsure why, white tigers tend to grow larger than orange ones.

While hunting, a tiger uses the whiskers on its snout to sense where it should bite its prey.

Sights and Sounds

During the day, tigers can see almost as well as humans can. At night, though, they have much better vision than people do. Like all jungle cats, tigers have huge round pupils that let in a lot of light. There is also a special structure at the back of a tiger's eye that helps it see better in the dark. These features give the tiger excellent night vision.

Tigers can hear a much broader range of sounds than people can. They rely on this excellent hearing to locate prey or other tigers. For instance, when a female tiger is ready to **mate** and a male tiger is far away, she might roar to get his attention. A tiger's roar is so loud that humans can hear it from up to 2 miles (3 km) away.

FUN FACT! Tigers have white spots on the backs of their ears that look like a second set of eyes. These spots trick prey into thinking that tigers can see in both directions.

A tiger opens its mouth wide to unleash its mighty roar.

CHAPTER 3

A Tiger's Lonesome Life

Tigers are mostly solitary animals. They spend very little time around other tigers. This is especially true of male tigers. A tiger's **territory** can cover hundreds of square miles. Tigers that live where food is scarce usually have larger territories than tigers that live where food is plentiful.

Female tigers aren't as protective of their territory as males are. It is not unusual for them to share territory with male tigers. This doesn't mean that male and female tigers live together as families, though. They usually only come together when the female is ready to mate. Once in a while, they might share a meal. On very rare occasions, they might even work together to take down prey. Most of the time, however, they avoid each other and mind their own business.

An adult tiger can go a very long time without coming into contact with another tiger.

Sniffing for Clues

Tigers have scent glands in their face, between their toes, and under their tail. They rub these body parts on trees and bushes to communicate with other tigers.

Tigers then use their sense of smell to collect information about other tigers. Male tigers know which areas belong to other males because they can smell the urine and droppings used to mark territory. Male tigers often fight to take territory away from each other. Sometimes they even fight to the death.

Male tigers also use their nose to find female tigers that are ready to mate. A male tiger finds a female by taking a strong breath near the markings she has left. This breath forces air into an area at the roof of the tiger's mouth called the Jacobson's organ. This organ sends a message to the tiger's brain telling it that a female is near.

Male tigers will stop at nothing to defend their territory from other males.

Tiger Cubs

Female tigers are first ready to mate when they are around three years old. They roar or leave scent messages to attract males.

It takes about three and a half months after mating for a litter of cubs to be born. Most litters have three cubs, but there can be as few as two or as many as seven.

Newborn cubs are tiny and defenseless. They depend entirely on their mothers for protection and food. They weigh only about 2 to 4 pounds (1 to 2 kg) at birth and are blind. Baby tigers are not able to see until they are around a week old. Their first food is milk from their mother. When a mother tiger goes to find food for herself, she is careful to hide her cubs from hungry animals. Even adult male tigers can be dangerous to a cub!

When the mother needs to move her babies from one place to another, she usually picks them up in her mouth. This might look painful, but it doesn't hurt the cubs at all.

Mother tigers gently pick up their cubs by the skin of the neck.

Teaching Cubs to Survive

After a few months, the mother begins to feed her cubs meat. The cubs grow very quickly. A cub might weigh as much as 180 pounds (82 kg) by the time it is one year old. Tiger cubs start to join their mother on hunts when they are between 8 and 10 months old. They learn the hunting skills they will need as adults by watching her stalk prey. They also practice their hunting skills by playing roughly with each other.

Cubs leave their mothers and go out on their own when they are between two and three years old. Male cubs find their own territory. Females sometimes end up staying close to their mothers. Sometimes they even share a part of their mother's territory.

Wild tigers live to be about 11 years old on average. Tigers in zoos sometimes live longer.

Tiger cubs often play by pretending to fight each other.

CHAPTER 4

Tigers Past and Present

Tigers are members of the cat family. Scientists believe that the earliest ancestors of today's cats roamed the earth about 37 million years ago.

One ancestor is known as the saber-toothed cat. Many people call these ancient animals saber-toothed tigers, but they were actually an entirely different type of cat. Saber-toothed cats died out thousands of years ago. We don't know exactly what they looked like. We do know that they were shorter than many of today's tigers, but probably heavier. We also know they had huge teeth that were up to 8 inches (20 cm) long. Scientists have learned most of what they know about saber-toothed cats by studying fossils.

Saber-toothed cats had incredibly large teeth.

Saber-toothed Cat

Diet: Carnivore (Meat Ea
Teeth: Incisors, Canines
Habitat: Some lived in fo

31

Siberians, Sumatrans, and Bengals

Today, there are six subspecies of tiger. All six are considered to be endangered.

Siberian tigers are the largest of all tiger subspecies. They can grow to be 11 feet (3 m) long and weigh up to 660 pounds (300 kg). Between 350 and 400 live in the cold forests of Siberia. Some might also live in northern China and North Korea.

Sumatrans are the smallest subspecies of tiger. They weigh between 200 and 265 pounds (91 and 120 kg) and are between 7 and 8 feet (2 and 2.4 m) long. These tigers are only found on the island of Sumatra. There are fewer than 500 living in the wild.

Bengal tigers live in the forests of several Asian countries. Their numbers have been decreasing rapidly since the early 2000s, but they are still the most common tiger subspecies. The Bengal is between 7 and 10 feet (2 and 3 m) long and weighs between 240 and 500 pounds (109 and 227 kg).

Sumatran tigers do not grow quite as large as other tiger subspecies do, but they are still bigger than most other cats.

The Rarest Tigers

Indo-Chinese tigers are much rarer than Bengals. They are found in Thailand, Cambodia, Myanmar, Laos, Vietnam, and Malaysia. These tigers weigh between 250 and 400 pounds (113 and 181 kg). There are only about 300 of them left in the wild.

In 2004, scientists decided that smaller Indo-Chinese tigers were actually a separate subspecies. They named this new subspecies the Malayan tiger. About 500 Malayan tigers live in southern Thailand and Malaysia.

The South China tiger is the rarest subspecies. In fact, it is almost extinct. No one has seen this subspecies in the wild for many years. There are about 50 of them living in zoos in China. South China tigers weigh between 200 and 400 pounds (91 and 181 kg) and are between 7 and 9 feet (2 and 2.7 m) long.

There are not many Indo-Chinese tigers left in the wild.

Tiger Relatives

Today, wild cats are native to every continent except for Australia and Antarctica. In addition to tigers, the cat family includes pumas, lions, leopards, cheetahs, and house cats. These cats come in a wide variety of sizes and colors, but they all have some things in common. They are all good hunters and have excellent hearing. They communicate using sounds and territory marks. They have five toes or claws on their front feet and four on their back feet. Most cats like to live on their own. Lions are a notable exception. They live in groups known as prides.

Each type of cat also has unique characteristics. Cheetahs are the fastest animals on land. Some cheetahs can run 70 miles (113 km) per hour. Leopards and pumas are both amazing long jumpers.

FUN FACT! Polydactyl cats, also known as mitten cats, have one or two extra toes on each of their feet.

Lions are closely related to tigers.

CHAPTER 5

Making the World Safe for Tigers

In the early 1900s, there were almost 100,000 tigers living in the wild. Today, there may be fewer than 4,000. In fact, more tigers live in captivity than in jungles and forests. How did this happen?

Humans have hunted and killed many tigers. Some were killed because they attacked livestock and people. Thousands were killed simply for sport. In the last century, three subspecies of tigers (Caspian, Bali, and Javan) were hunted to extinction.

Many countries have outlawed tiger hunting and created safe areas for tigers to live, but this has not stopped the killing. A single tiger pelt can bring a poacher tens of thousands of dollars. Some people also purchase tiger body parts. They believe the body parts can be used to cure everything from arthritis to skin problems. This has not been proven to be correct, but it makes it very tempting for poachers to kill tigers.

Poached tiger pelts are often used as decorative objects.

Disappearing Homes

Tiger populations are also decreasing because of **habitat** loss. As people clear land for farms and factories, there is less room for tigers to live and hunt.

Many groups have tried to help tigers. On the Chinese calendar, 2010 was the Year of the Tiger. That year, there was a special meeting in Russia for representatives from the 13 countries where tigers live in the wild. The countries agreed to try to double the wild tiger population by 2022, the next Year of the Tiger.

It will not be easy to fix the problems of poaching and habitat loss. But if people work together, they can help tigers live safely in the wild for years to come.

FUN FACT! A 1970 law made it illegal to shoot tigers in India.

We must work hard to ensure that tigers will always have space to live and grow.

Words to Know

camouflage (KAM-o-flaj) — coloring or body shape that allows an animal to blend in with its surroundings

captivity (kap-TIV-i-tee) — the condition of being held or trapped by people

carnivores (KAR-nih-vorz) — animals that have meat as a regular part of their diet

climates (KLYE-mitz) — the weather typical of places over long periods of time

continent (KAHN-tuh-nuhnt) — one of the seven large landmasses of the earth

cubs (KUBZ) — baby tigers

endangered (en-DAYN-jurd) — at risk of becoming extinct, usually because of human activity

extinct (ik-STINGKT) — no longer found alive

habitat (HAB-uh-tat) — the place where an animal or plant is usually found

litter (LIT-ur) — a number of baby animals that are born at the same time to the same mother

mate (MAYT) — to join together to produce babies

pelt (PELT) — an animal's skin with the hair or fur still on it

poacher (POH-chur) — a person who hunts or fishes illegally

predators (PREH-duh-turz) — animals that live by hunting other animals for food

prey (PRAY) — an animal that's hunted by another animal for food

retract (ree-TRAKT) — to pull inside

subspecies (SUHB-spee-sheez) — groups of animals that are part of the same species, but are different in some important ways

territory (TER-i-tor-ee) — area of land claimed by an animal

vertebrates (VER-tuh-bruts) — animals that have a backbone

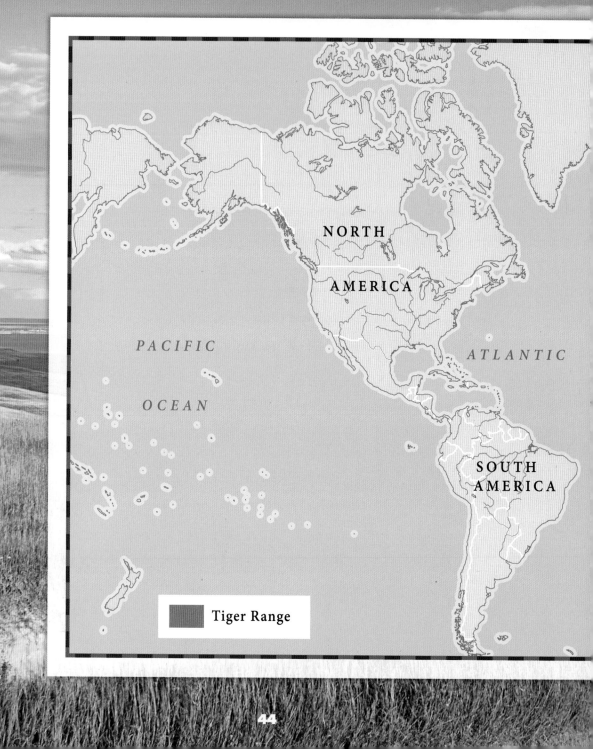

NORTH

AMERICA

PACIFIC

ATLANTIC

OCEAN

SOUTH
AMERICA

Tiger Range

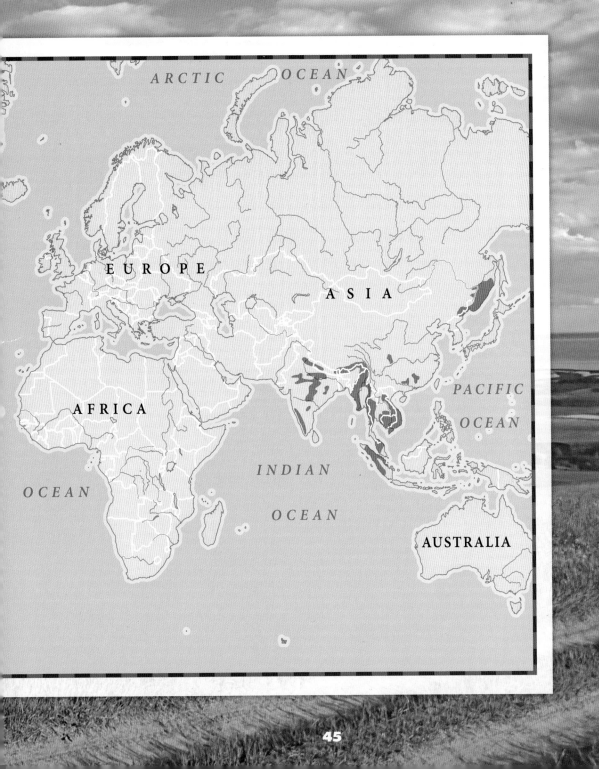

ARCTIC OCEAN

EUROPE

ASIA

AFRICA

PACIFIC OCEAN

OCEAN

INDIAN

OCEAN

AUSTRALIA

Find Out More

Books

Jenkins, Martin. *Can We Save the Tiger?* Somerville, MA: Candlewick Press, 2011.

Marsh, Laura. *Tigers*. Washington, D.C.: National Geographic, 2012.

O'Brien, Patrick. *Sabertooth*. New York: Henry Holt and Company, 2008.

Wilsdon, Christina. *Tigers*. Pleasantville, NY: Reader's Digest Young Families, 2006.

Visit this Scholastic Web site for more information on tigers:
www.factsfornow.scholastic.com
Enter the keyword **Tiger**

Index

About the Author

Vicky Franchino has written dozens of books for children. She was surprised to learn that there are no wild tigers in Africa (!) and sad to find out that all tigers are in danger of extinction. Vicky lives in Madison, Wisconsin, with her husband and daughters. She likes to visit her local zoo—Vilas Zoo—which is home to a Siberian tiger.